The
Rabbit
in the
Garden

by **Dana Meachen Rau**

Reading Consultant: Nanci R. Vargus, Ed. D.

 Marshall Cavendish
Benchmark
New York

Picture Words

bat

bean

crickets

ears

fox

frog

garden

grass

legs

lettuce

moon

owl

plants

rabbit

rabbit's

3

A  has slept in the all day.

Now the is ready to eat.

The  is out.

The  hops to the

.

The  is full of
to eat.

The nibbles on
some .

The  hears a croak.

The  hears the chirp.

An and a
fly through the sky.

They come out at night,
too.

The  eats leaves.

Then the  stops and waits.

The 's long  hear a sound.

A  is creeping closer.

The  hops out of
the .

The 's  help it
hop far and fast.

The  cannot find
the 🐇.

The 🐇 is hiding in
the tall ████.

Challenge Words

chirp   (churp)
the sound a cricket makes

creeping (KREEP-ing)
walking slowly and carefully

croak   (krohk)
the sound a frog makes

nibbles   (NIB-ulz)
takes small bites

Find Out More

Books

Ganeri, Anita. *Rabbits*. Chicago, IL: Heinemann Library, 2003.

Hibbert, Clare. *Rabbit*. Mankato, MN: Smart Apple Media, 2005.

Holub, Joan. *Why Do Rabbits Hop?* New York: Dial Books for Young Readers, 2003.

Rayner, Matthew. *Rabbit*. Milwaukee, WI: Gareth Stevens Publishing, 2004.

Videos

See How They Grow: Wild Animals, Sony Wonder.

Web Sites

Division of Fish and Wildlife
http://www.in.gov/dnr/fishwild/publications/lifeseries/rabbit.htm

Nature Haven
http://www.naturehaven.com/rabbit.html

Smithsonian National Zoological Park
http://nationalzoo.si.edu

23

About the Author

Dana Meachen Rau is an author, editor, and illustrator. A graduate of Trinity College in Hartford, Connecticut, she has written more than one hundred books for children, including nonfiction, biographies, early readers, and historical fiction. She spots rabbits in her backyard garden in Burlington, Connecticut, in the early morning.

About the Reading Consultant

Nanci R. Vargus, Ed.D, wants all children to enjoy reading. She used to teach first grade. Now she works at the University of Indianapolis. Nanci helps young people become teachers. Rabbits sometimes nibble the vegetables in her Indianapolis garden.

Marshall Cavendish Benchmark
99 White Plains Road
Tarrytown, NY 10591-9001
www.marshallcavendish.us

Copyright © 2007 by Marshall Cavendish Corporation
All rights reserved.
No part of this book may be reproduced in any form without written consent of the publisher.

All Internet sites were correct at the time of printing.

Library of Congress Cataloging-In-Data

Rau, Dana Meachen, 1971–
The rabbit in the garden / by Dana Meachen Rau.
    p. cm. — (Benchmark rebus)
Summary: "A rebus book about a rabbit that finds dinner in a garden"—Provided by publisher.
Includes bibliographical references.
ISBN-13: 978-0-7614-2308-9
ISBN-10: 0-7614-2308-7
Rabbits—Juvenile literature. I. Title. II. Series.
QL737.L3R38 2006
599.32—dc22
        2005029050

Editor: Christine Florie
Editorial Director: Michelle Bisson
Art Director: Anahid Hamparian
Series Designer: Virginia Pope

Photo research by Connie Gardner
Rebus images provided courtesy of *Dorling Kindersley*.

Cover photo by Konrad Wothe/Minden Pictures

The photographs in this book are used with permission and through the courtesy of:
Corbis: p. 5 Herbert Kehrer/zefa; p. 7 Royalty-Free; p. 15 H. Spichtinger/zefa; p. 19 Jose Fuste Raga/zefa; *Getty*: p. 9;
Peter Arnold: p. 11 R. Andrew Odum; *DRK Photo*: p. 13 Joe McDonald; *Photo Researchers*: p. 17 Steve and Dave
Maslowski; *Minden Pictures*: p. 21 Jim Brandenburg.

Printed in Malaysia
1 3 5 6 4 2